April 2023

Linda – Thank
such a friendly and cheerful
neighbor. You have brought
a bright light into our
neighborhood.

Many Blessings

Joci

The Gathering of One

of One

The **ART** of
CREATING MORE
PEACE and **JOY**
IN YOUR LIFE

REVEREND
JOIE BARRY

BookBaby, 7905 N Route 130, Pennsauken, NJ 08110, store.bookbaby.com

Ordering Information:

For details, contact thegatheringofone@outlook.com

Print ISBN: 978-1-66788-152-2 eBook ISBN: 978-1-66788-153-9

Printed in the United States of America on SFI Certified paper.

Photo: Donna Willingham Iobst

The Gathering Of One Logo Design: Terri Bridgwater

First Edition: 2023

TABLE OF CONTENTS

INTRODUCTION

Dear Ones,

For several years, I created and led an inter-faith, inter-spiritual group called The Gathering of One. We gathered every few months and focused on a different religion or spiritual practice including Islam, Judaism, Sacred Sound, Singing Bowls, Native American Spirituality, and Christianity, to name only a few. We meditated, prayed, stomped, sang, hummed, questioned, and listened. More importantly, we learned and grew, and we became more tolerant and accepting of the sacred practices and rituals of others.

The name for this group came to me when my sister read about a structure being built in Berlin called The House of One. It was to be the world's first house of prayer for three religions, containing a church, a mosque, and a synagogue. Up until this point, I had been calling my future group The Gathering, and it now made sense to call it The Gathering of One.

Like many other things in our world, The Gathering of One ended when the COVID-19 pandemic began and the outlet for my soul's yearnings came to an end. In its place came a beautiful time of introspection and spiritual growth for my Soul. Rather than researching, organizing, and presenting, I went within reading, listening, praying, meditating, and writing.

For the past two years, the voice of Spirit has been flowing through me and the following reflections are the results of this Divine flow. Many of these reflections have been shared and recorded under the title "Dear

Ones" on daily social media postings, while others have only been recorded in my private journal.

What I write and post are known as lojongs or mind training, a contemplative Tibetan Buddhist practice that makes use of lists of aphorisms, affirmations, or slogans to purify one's motivations and attitudes. They are designed as antidotes to undesired mental habits that cause suffering. One of the most well known teachers who uses this practice is Pema Chodron.

Many years ago, a psychic told me that I had a book inside me that needed to come out. At that time, I had no inkling of writing a book and pretty much dismissed her prediction. I now clearly remember her saying to me again as I walked out her door, "Please make sure that you write that book. It's alive inside of you and it's very important for you to birth it." So, here it is!

My purpose for writing this book is to help you lead a more peaceful and joy-filled life. Life is hard. But there are ways to create a simpler and easier life while we are in this physical body and on this earth.

I pray that my reflections are of some assistance to you in your spiritual journey. Feel free to utilize this book in whatever way works best for you. You can work through it chapter by chapter or jump to a chapter that speaks to you right now.

At the end of each chapter, I have included references to books, YouTube videos, articles, and podcasts that I believe may be helpful to you on your spiritual journey. I have only included those that I believe are worthwhile and powerful, so please take the time to watch, read, listen, write, and reflect.

Love and blessings,
Reverend Joie Barry

CHAPTER ONE:

HOW TO LIVE BY SPIRITUAL LAWS

During a painful and nasty divorce, I began searching for something that would help me make sense of what was happening to me in the emotional and physical world. My sister and I had attended several events, including presentations by Wayne Dyer sponsored by the local Unity Church and, eventually, I found my way to Unity of Lehigh Valley in Emmaus. Of course, "On the Way to Emmaus." This is where I heard for the first time about spiritual laws. I became curious about them and have since studied and practiced them for years.

Here are some of my favorites. I know there are many spiritual laws and truths I haven't included. Feel free to take the time to add your own laws and truths in your journal entries.

How to practice and live by Spiritual Laws:

- If you desire grace, practice grace and be gracious.
- If you want to live in faith, judge by faith and be faithful.
- If you want to have friends, be friendly with yourself and then with others. Time spent with friends is a sacred space. Be grateful when you have the opportunity and make the experience worthwhile by being positive and hopeful. Bless your friends and do it often.
- If you want more patience, be patient with yourself first and you will have more patience with others.
- If you want to be heard, be a good listener.

- If you are looking for love, love yourself and then be lovely to others.

- If you want success, freedom, love, and peace, send out the same to everyone around you and all this and more will come to you.

- If you want harmony in your life, spread the seeds of kindness, gentleness, love, peace, and hope, and you will receive the same in return.

- If you want to stay young at heart, be friendly, helpful, and loving. You are only as young or as old as your heart's purpose tells you that you are.

- If you want to be filled with joy, be cheerful, be positive, be prayerful, and sing and dance often.

- If you want to receive, you must give first. When we give love, we receive life. When we give of ourselves, we receive grace.

- You reap what you sow. This is a basic and familiar spiritual law. It reminds us to be careful about how we treat ourselves, others, and our planet. Smile and be joyful, and the world will rally around you. Frown and be miserable, and you will frown alone. So go the laws of the Universe.

The Law of Attraction

What we think, how we live, what we do, how we act, and what we say becomes our soul-body. That is Divine Law! We draw to us what we think and talk about all day long. Watch what you are thinking and saying closely so you only attract good into your life. Let's think and talk about abundance, safety, serving, and caring for one another, then watch as you attract these desirable things into your world. Live from the inside out by choosing and focusing on what you want, not what you don't want. Then add the right actions to your thoughts.

The Law of Attraction states that everything that happens in our physical world happens in our minds first. First, we have the thought and then we have the experience.

When we send out thoughts about someone else, they receive them and these thoughts will manifest and return to us. Remember this when you think about others and be careful and thoughtful in all your activities. Work on bringing out the best in yourself, and in response, the best in others.

Wherever You Go, There You Are! Everywhere you are is exactly where you are supposed to be, and, therefore, Sacred Space.

The Law of Giving and Receiving

Be generous with your time, talent, resources, and gifts. Give freely and profusely. Give more of everything than necessary or expected. Do you ever feel unworthy when someone is generous toward you? Remember, with the law of giving and receiving that someone needs to be the receiver. Be not only a generous giver, but also a gracious receiver. When someone gives you a gift, all you need to do is say "Thank you!"

The Laws of Grace and Mercy

Beyond the natural law of Karma, there are also the laws of Grace and Mercy. Grace is a Divine dispensation of mercy and the unearned gift of Higher Love. It dissolves karma, creates miracles, and can change physical matter. Depending upon the situation, ask for grace and mercy in your life.

The Law of Creation

The Creative Process is the energy of thoughts held in mind that, when properly nourished thru prayer and meditation, will move into physical reality and produce in kind.

The Law of Perpetual Motion

All things come in cycles. Everything is moving and nothing is permanent. In good times, enjoy what you have while it lasts. If things are negative, prepare yourself for a prosperous change coming your way.

The Law of Polarity or Opposites

When we are going through difficult times, there is always something good waiting for us on the other side. There are two types of energy. These two types of energy are often described as feminine/masculine, yin/yang, or anima/animus. Everyone possesses all of these energies. Our challenge is to achieve a balance between them. If you live facing the Light, shadows fall behind you. If you live turned away from the Light, there is nothing but shadows. Be sure to be turned toward the Light!

The Law of Divine Oneness

Absolutely everything in our universe is interconnected. Every word, belief, action, and choice you make has an impact on the world. Muslims call this tauheed.

The Law of Relativity

Everything is neutral when viewed in isolation. Nothing is good or bad until we begin to compare it with something else.

Love Your Higher Power, Love Yourself, Love Your Neighbor

Almost every major religion or spiritual practice advocates this law. Create a loving and intimate relationship with your higher power. Next, take care of your personal needs and the needs of your family. Then, offer service and kindness to others. Loving others is a Spiritual responsibility.

One Can Be in the World, But Not of the World

This is not easy to do, but it is still possible. Practice non-attachment. Feel free to use the good things of this world and, when you are done with them, release them for others to use. Listen to Truth when it calls to you to come out of your world and into Spirit's world.

Make the World a Better Place

As each one of us does our special work using our unique gifts and skills, the world becomes a better place. Know and live your spiritual mission, and Spirit's purpose will be accomplished and lives will be changed for the better.

Everything Has a Beginning and an Ending

Since everything has a beginning and an ending, if it isn't good, then it isn't over. When things are not going well, remember that eventually this will come to an end and only good will prevail. Rejoice and be glad in it.

Cause and Effect

Things never happen by chance in this material world, there are causes and effects. Sometimes there might be accidents, but in the material world, even so-called accidents have their cause and effect.

We Are Created Whole and Healthy

Join me in imagining a world where we are all living in peak health, a world where we use light and love to heal ourselves. Anything we can imagine, we can create. Since we are created in the image of Spirit, we come into this world whole and healthy. Focus on returning to this Truth, no matter what your current health circumstances may be telling you. When we give a name to an illness, we give power to it and reinforce or feed the dis-ease. Speak only words of healing and perfect health, and join me in seeing a world free from dis-ease, and free from all pain and suffering.

Choose wholeness! See yourself as well, fine, and perfect. Imagine that you are in excellent health—physically, mentally, and spiritually—now and forevermore. And so it will be!

See The Truth All Around You

Open your eyes and see The Truth. What use is a tree without fruit? Don't be a fruitless disappointment. When you see an opportunity, get involved and offer to help. It is not what you do, but who you are that counts. This shines through—who you are—much more than what you say or do.

Free Will

We all possess Free Will. We can use our Will to disregard Divine Law and bring chaos and destruction into our world, or we can use our Will to follow and bless the laws and bring order out of chaos. It's up to us to choose. Focus on developing patience and humor. We are the only creatures on earth given the gift of personal choice. Choose creativity and laughter!

As a Spiritual Being, You Are Free

Know the Truth, that you are a spiritual being and you will be free. Take Radical Responsibility for every area of your life, from your relationships to your work life to your health and finances. This is not a burden, it is very freeing.

Anything not in activity enters into separation, commonly known as death. It's an ever-changing world. Stay active, happy, and joyous. Expand your energy and continue to grow. It will improve your condition and the conditions of everyone around you.

QUESTIONS AND INSIGHTS TO JOURNAL ABOUT SPIRITUAL LAWS

1. Many of us are great givers, but struggle at being gracious receivers. How good are you at being a receiver?

2. Do you truly believe that everything that comes into your life is for your good?

3. I awoke one morning with the word "Truth" on my tongue. What is your Truth? How do you find your Truth? There are lots of questions, and you can fill your days searching for the answers.

4. How good are you at helping others and being kind to everyone you meet? What are some specific things you can do to improve in these areas?

5. Do you accept responsibility for the power of your thoughts, words, and actions? If not, what steps can you take to improve in this area?

6. Are you a Wise One (sometimes referred to as old souls, wizards, witches, priests/priestesses, psychics, spiritual or energy healers, medicine men/women or sorcerers)? If you believe that you are a Wise One, what does that mean to you?

7. What are your thoughts about accidents and coincidences?

8. Have you ever experienced the Law of Love, either in the giving or receiving of it? If so, what was that experience like?

9. Since everything that manifests in our physical world happens in our minds first, are you capable of entertaining thoughts without accepting or manifesting them?

Resources
Listen to Linda Graham on Resilience:
https://www.oneyoufeed.net/?s=Linda+graham

The Law of Love: The action of freely giving without any expectation of manifestation, reward, or receiving anything in return for that which was given.

CHAPTER TWO:
FINDING FAITH IN EVERYDAY LIFE

All my life, I have had a deep sense of faith and connection. As a young child, I had an ongoing and two-way conversation with an imaginary friend who I realized as an adult was Spirit. This conversation has been my guiding light, and has given me a deep understanding of faith.

One might think that growing up in the Catholic Church would have been a challenge for a child who talks to and listens to Spirit. Interestingly, it was not. The Church provided me with a place where others sang, worshiped, and prayed just as I did, and it gave me the tools and the words to interact more deeply with my friend, Spirit.

The doctrine and teachings of the Catholic Church did not speak to me when I became an adult, and that eventually caused me to leave. To this day, I am still very comfortable attending a wedding, funeral, or Mass, and can easily flow right back into the always-comforting rituals of the Catholic Church.

Here's a funny story about going to confession: As a young and very obedient child, I had a difficult time coming up with sins to confess, and I never really believed that I needed to confess anything to a priest. So, I would make up sins. My favorite one was that I fought with my sister. Since we never fought, I now had another sin to confess: I lied! But I did love having all those required prayers (penance) to repeat after my short and contrived confessions.

For all of its shortcomings, the Catholic Church helped me put into perspective what I was experiencing as a child: the light and love of God.

Whether we are consciously aware of it or not, we are always walking in the light. The challenge is becoming aware of it, seeing everyone around you also walking in the light, and having faith that this is the Truth. In the beginning, the Creator said, "Let there be light." You, dear one, are one of those lights.

We have come together for a reason. Live from your highest purpose, shine your light, and freely share your love and life with your family, friends, pets, and everyone and everything around you.

You are not a square peg in a round hole. You are right where you are supposed to be. Make yourself fit into the hole you're in! Have faith!

I am the light of the world. You are the light of the world.

Believe in the light, and all will be well. Remember that you are Spirit's candle. You are made to shine, not just today but every day. Let your love and patience flow. Let your light shine into the lives of those you meet day-by-day, bringing hope and love to the world. Allow your heart to sing and your face to be warmed by the light of Spirit so you may meet your needs and overcome all challenges. Find the calm that brings you peace and happiness in your daily life. And light your candles every day!

Speak gently and kindly to those who falter. We cannot know another's struggles, only our own. Pray that the light will shine in everyone's lives as it does in yours.

It's best not to hide from our sadness. Better to face it bravely and allow Spirit to help us work through it. Light and love are waiting for us on the other side.

Get out of your boat and walk on the water. Get out of your comfort zone and do what you are being called to do. You already know the way. Use your gifts to help others in need. It's why you are here. Have patient endurance, which means tending to your heart's garden and watering it with love.

Let go, Let God. We hear these sayings all the time: One day at a time; be a channel for good; be a blessing to the world; put feet to your prayers and dreams; and cooperate with and lift up others. But if you live these truisms, your life will be more fulfilling.

Sow your seeds. Now is the time to have faith in Spirit by tending to your tiny seeds so you can reap the fruits in the future. Just don't forget to water and weed them.

Have faith in your Creator. Have faith in yourself and others, and don't forget to be sweet. Help those who are weaker in mind, body, or spirit. Someone needs to stay uplifted and set the example for others to follow. That someone is you! Such is the challenge facing light workers like us. Know who you are spiritually, mentally, emotionally, and physically. Allow your life to be an example for others to follow. Always remember, what you do to others, you do to the Divine.

As your faith grows, you will understand more about life and will find that life gets easier. Seek out Spirit throughout your day, and you will be amply rewarded. Having a strong faith not only makes your Spirit stronger, it makes your mind and body stronger as well. As your desire for physical things lessens, your spiritual desires will become stronger.

As a spiritual being, you are free and unlimited. What if you believed that your life is filled with magic and miracles, and that is all that can happen to you? Maybe everything in your life would get better. Seek out this magic and become a beacon of light for this world. Light and love will draw near to you, as you are always one with Spirit. Keep as much sunshine in your life as possible.

QUESTIONS AND INSIGHTS TO JOURNAL ABOUT FAITH

1. Do you believe that you are the light of the world? What does that look like for you? How do you show up in this world as the light?

2. Can there be light without darkness? How do you see the connection between light and darkness?

3. Does the light shine in your world? How can you help to shine this light in the world for others?

4. Do you light your own candles or do you expect others to light them for you?

5. How do you live out your faith? Are you thoughtful, joyous, helpful, trusting, caring, or something else?

6. What do you have faith in? How strong is your faith and how do you tend to it?

7. How strong is your prayer life? Are you confident that what you pray for is already happening even before you can see it in physical reality?

8. Do you tend to hide from sadness or difficulties? If so, what are some ways that can help you face your emotions more honestly?

9. Can you get out of your boat and walk on the water? What does this mean to you and how can you go about doing it?

10. Do you have Patient Endurance with yourself and others?

Resources
Watch on YouTube: **https://melrobbins.com/the-5-second-rule/**

May your light burn so brightly that it shines the way for those around you who are lost or stumbling.

CHAPTER THREE:

PRACTICING FORGIVENESS

Should I really include this here for the whole world to read? Well, why not? How can I write about love, courage, and forgiveness if I don't practice what I preach?

Once upon a time, I was married and I loved it! I loved being married, not necessarily the person I was married to. What I loved was the idea of being married, and I always thought I would be married for my entire life.

Well, Spirit had other ideas and my marriage of almost thirty years ended in a difficult and nasty divorce. It was almost a cliché as there was the other woman, who apparently was in the picture for more years than I care to admit.

Once I learned the real reason my former husband left, I went through a range of emotions, none of them good for me or anyone around me. It took years of therapy, prayer, dark nights of the soul, and forgiveness rituals before I finally realized the truth of this experience. It was a gift, the gift of freedom.

From the point of this realization to this very day, I am grateful for my many years of marriage, for my former husband, for the nasty divorce, and for the beautiful son we created. And, I am grateful for the deceit, lies, anger, and turmoil, all of which pushed me kicking and screaming on to this spiritual journey.

The saying "Turn the other cheek" literally means to turn away from evil. It's the spiritual practice of nonresistance and forgiveness. I often tell people that I am "Holding them in my heart," which is my way of telling them that I love them. It's also my way to forgive others without ever having to interact or speak with them. Forgiveness starts in your heart–mind, and does not need words or actions.

Have you or someone you love been hurt or rejected, and you felt the need for revenge? Try finding freedom in forgiveness. Even if your anger seems justifiable, douse the flames with holy water and move on. Follow the voice of Spirit.

Perfection – No one is perfect. There is no such thing as a person without faults. Strive to do your best, and then forgive yourself when you fall short and forgive others when they falter. Stop faultfinding, in both yourself and others. Practice patience in thought, word, and deed, and create a better world for all.

Let's all be a little more tolerant and patient. Not tolerant as in timid, but as in a willingness to accept the existence of opinions or behaviors that you don't necessarily agree with. Positive and consistent patience with yourself and others will create a better life for you and everyone around you. See only the good in others. Search for ways to say a kind word. Allow kindness, gentleness, and patience to be your guide. Treat everyone gently and kindly, as we never know what's going on in their lives. Always remember to look for what is beautiful and to search for ways to agree rather than disagree. Stay awake!

Wear your crown and shine your light. Reach out in kindness and see the worth in people's hearts. Pray for the light to shine in their hearts, and never be afraid to shine your light.

The Platinum Rule:

We all know the golden rule. However, since we are all different, I prefer the Platinum Rule: "Do unto others as they would want done unto them." (Dave Kerpen)

How often shall I forgive? Seven times? Yes, seventy times seven, until you may know what is really contained inside yourself. Only through patience come understanding and forgiveness. Remove yourself from criticizing and finding fault with others. Have patience in thought, word, and deed. This is the beginning of forgiveness, and the road to wisdom.

Be patient and kind always. Don't criticize yourself, and don't criticize others. What we criticize in others is a reflection of what we see in ourselves. We are always looking into a two-way mirror. Give yourself the gift of forgiveness and hold no grudges. Every day, we constantly meet ourselves. The hardships we blame on others are caused by ourselves. Understand that when you're meeting others, you're actually meeting yourself.

If you doubt whether good will come to you, you are right and already defeated. If you believe only good comes to you, you are on the right path. Do the right things—physically, mentally, and spiritually—and good will come to you. Right-side-up living means living with Truth and listening to the words of Spirit. Allow Spirit to illuminate and light up your path. Forgive yourself and others with ease and grace.

Guilt is a humbling and debilitating emotion. Release and forgive yourself today from any self-condemnation. Allow Spirit to protect your mind and emotions and to set you free from guilt. Be honest with yourself and it will naturally follow that you will be honest with others.

Forgiveness brings us freedom. Allow the Spirit within you to do the work of forgiveness, and you will become aware of all that is good, perfect, and pure. When you forgive, you become free.

Let go of envy. Allow your experience to be one of love and forgiveness. Let go of turmoil, drama, and attachment, so your activities work only toward good.

When someone draws a circle that seems to exclude you, try drawing your own circle and invite that person into it.

QUESTIONS AND INSIGHTS TO JOURNAL ABOUT FORGIVENESS

1. Describe a time when you had to "douse the flames with holy water?"

2. How quickly and easily do you forgive?

3. What does it mean to you to forgive seventy times seven?

4. Can you see beyond the physical appearances, actions, and words of others to see their true selves?

5. Have you or someone you love been hurt or rejected? How do you practice forgiveness when this happens?

6. Do you strive for perfection, or are you able to do your best and move on?

7. How patient are you? How can you practice being more patient?

8. What does it mean to look into a two-way mirror? Can you accept that you cannot see something in someone else unless it is already in you?

9. How do you respond when someone honestly questions or doubts you? Do you become defensive or do you invite the doubter in?

Resources
Listen to Brene Brown on Empathy
https://ed.ted.com/best_of_web/BXaLcbG4

Speak these words: "I release you and I let you go. You are free. I am free. And so it is!"

CHAPTER FOUR:

THE IMPORTANCE OF REST AND PLAY

It took me many years to come to a place where I could give myself permission to rest and relax, many years of pushing myself to finish my to-do list and get one more thing done before I would allow myself to rest or play.

To this day, I'm not sure why I had this internal drive to push myself and always do more. But, one day several years ago, I finally came to the realization that I am a human being and not a human doer.

I don't regret my many years of striving and over-doing, as it was the reason for my success in the material world that has allowed me the time and space to explore my inner spiritual world at this point in my life. It has also allowed me the opportunity to do things like write this book.

We all need to rest, play, and laugh much more often. Watch a funny movie or show, read some jokes, go see a live comedian, take a nap, and go to bed early or sleep late. Laugh at yourself, and laugh at and with life. Humor is a great healer. Be as active and upbeat as possible. Smile and laugh often. This will create a much better environment for the changes and influences swirling around you.

My prayer for you is that the line between your work and your play is so thin that you can't tell the difference.

I was introduced to Laughter Yoga during seminary. It is an exercise program for health and well-being. It's a combination of laughter exercises with yoga breathing techniques. Laughter releases endorphins, which are natural painkillers and can help with arthritis, spondylitis, chronic migraine headaches, chronic pain, fibromyalgia, and autoimmune and chronic inflammatory diseases.

A rousing, hearty laugh is good for the body, mind, and spirit. Find something every day that makes you laugh. If anyone laughs at you, laugh with them!

To learn more, check out the following website: **laughteryoga.org**

Join me in seeing a world where we are all in perfect health and harmony with Mother Earth. Let's see love, rest, laughter, and joy as the only medicine that we need. Allow yourself to express your feelings. God gave you the ability to not only laugh, but to cry as well. Do not suppress your God-given imaginative forces.

Staying busy is easy. Staying well rested is the challenge. It's important to keep your energy, happiness, creativity, and relationships fresh and thriving amid the never-ending family demands, career pressures, and the stress of everyday life. Take some time each day to just watch your thoughts, allowing them to flow freely. Do not accept or reject them, just observe them. Write down some of the thoughts you have observed and how you felt while doing this exercise. It will make for an interesting day, I promise!

Spirit wants us to live a well-rounded and centered life. Every week, take time to work and play, exercise and rest, eat and fast, study and meditate, laugh and cry, talk and be quiet, and make yourself holy and pray for others. If you are worried or stressed, try relaxing in a hot tub full of water, and all of your cares will bubble up and float away.

Life is more worthwhile when we are consistent. Not just persistent but consistent in every area of our lives—in work and play and with our family, friends, and fellow travelers.

Spirit sees us exactly as who we really are: unique, beautiful, and precious. During times of stress or sadness, rest in this knowledge of infinite love.

Take time to rest in the sun. Listen and sing along to the music. Stay close to nature. Watch the sun rise and set. Hear the bees buzzing and the birds singing. Touch the earth and smell the flowers. Life is short—enjoy every precious minute of it!

Care for your body temple, as it houses your Spirit. Feed your body temple healthy and nutritious food. Exercise, rest, and practice deep breathing. To obtain perfect health, spend time in nature, laugh often, enjoy your family and friends, and love and cherish yourself.

Rest is the way you obtain the refill of energy that you need. Make sure you get the right kind of rest, or you will feel empty. Take care of yourself by keeping your mind focused on Spirit. Do not overcommit yourself. This practice will help you live a life free of fear and pain.

Work, play, rest, and place your faith in Spirit. Stay awake and aware of the Divine Life within you and within everyone you see. By doing this, you will experience much more joy in your activities.

Don't try to do too much. It's only our material laws that make us believe that we have to work hard. Leave something for God to do!

QUESTIONS AND INSIGHTS TO JOURNAL ABOUT REST AND PLAY

1. How do you play?

2. What does fun mean to you, and what do you do to have fun?

3. How often do you truly laugh? What makes you laugh? How can you find ways to laugh more often?

4. Is it possible for you to laugh at yourself and at life in general?

5. Can you see the humorous side in almost every experience? Nothing in this world is good or bad, only our judging makes them so. Try to analyze every experience from all angles until you can see the humor in it.

6. Do you feel that you are in harmony with Mother Earth? If not, what are some things you can do to increase this possibility?

7. Try envisioning a world where sickness and dis-ease don't exist because we are too busy singing and dancing with Spirit, reveling in our perfection. Write down your thoughts about what this world would look like for you.

8. How in touch do you believe you are with your feelings and emotions? Become conscious of when you laugh and try to count how many times you laugh on a given day. On the flip side, how often do you cry?

9. Take some time—a day or even a few hours—to just watch your thoughts, allowing them to flow freely. Do not accept or reject them, just observe them. Write down some of the thoughts you have observed and how you felt doing this exercise.

10. Eliminate some things from your to-do list today and use your newfound time to help or be kind to someone in need.

11. Do you have one day each week where you hold the Sabbath? It's important to give yourself a day of rest and reflection, as it will allow you to return to your busy life with renewed energy and purpose. Take a few minutes every day to steal away to a quiet place and commune with Spirit and replenish your soul.

Resources

Listen to these podcasts:

https://podcasts.apple.com/us/podcast/fun-what-the-hell-is-it-and-why-do-we-need-it/ https://brenebrown.com/podcast/on-my-mind-rbg-surge-capacity-and-play-as-an-energy-source/

Take this quiz: https://www.restquiz.com/quiz/rest-quiz-test/

Keep the faith!

CHAPTER FIVE:

INNER STRENGTH

So, I had to search my inner being to determine how I have personally become so strong. I do not mean physically strong, as I have never been a physically strong woman, but emotionally and spiritually strong.

People often ask me how I appear to stay so calm when there is turmoil going on around me. It's a good question, and when I look inside I realize that I don't just appear to be calm, internally I feel calm and at peace.

Spending time alone in prayer and meditation has brought me to a deep place of serenity and peace. Working through the pain of realizing I had lived for many years in the land of deceit and coming through to the other side has helped to make me strong.

Realizing that it was the deceitfulness and not the ending of a marriage that totally crushed me, being willing to work through that with the help of an excellent therapist, and the discovery of an inner spiritual world has made me strong.

In this chapter, I wish to share with you how you might deepen your spiritual gifts of strength and power. Not the physically strong or egotistical type of power but the quiet inner strength that resides in all of us. Right now, we all need to tap into our inner powers and use them for the greater good. This is where your true power resides. Listen closely to your still, small voice within, have faith, and allow your Spirit to fly freely.

When you know your spiritual strength, life becomes more effortless and you become more non-resistant. You will gain an internal sense of the strength that brings you joy and that no one can take away or even disturb within you.

My superpower is listening. I have a very acute sense of hearing, which at times can be so annoying that I need to tune things out. When I relax into my superpower and accept it as the gift that it is, I end up enjoying all of the many sounds and voices that are only mine to hear and learn from.

Let your light, love, and patience shine in the lives of all you meet. Allow your light to shine so others may find their way. Be intentional with your yeses and your noes. Do not become weary and discouraged. Look up and lift up your voice and your eyes to the Divine. Ask Spirit for strength, and be filled with joy as you serve. Stay joyous in the wonders of life. May your mind be open and your heart glad for a purpose or a cause that is important to you. Spirit will support you and make you strong for the causes that align with it. Let all you do be done in order and harmony. And for God's sake, be joyous!

So, I've been told to be a rock. A rock for myself and for everyone around me in what sometimes appears to be—in the outer world—a crumbling situation. If this makes any sense to you, come and join me. Together we can create a pile of solid and sturdy rocks for the world to build on.

Be patient with yourself and with others. Through patience, you will find strength within yourself and will express love and hope to others.

My heart is softening and my compassion is deepening as I observe the dreams and hopes of myself and others. I look at the world with peace, love, and compassion, and see it reflected back to me. I see you! Just for today, see people for who they really are and invite them in.

Strength comes in many different forms. Being true to yourself is an important piece of self-love. We cannot be true to others until we are first true to ourselves. It's important to streamline your day, as you can only make a certain number of good decisions in a day's time. So, make important decisions when you are most alert. For most of us that's earlier in the day. Make the first hour and the last hour of each day the best times of your day. Guard your heart and your mind from negative thoughts and people. Don't allow others to change or alter your beliefs. Align your heart and mind with the Holy Spirit.

Self-discipline is another form of strength. When you find yourself faltering or feeling weak, say to yourself, "I love you too much to allow you to do or to not do that."

Be very careful about pretending to be someone you're not, as you will eventually become who you are pretending to be. Be not afraid of being and showing to the world who you really are. Who you really are is a gift to the world. Place your trust in the Creator and not in yourself or others. Don't be afraid of what others might say or do. Live your life with courage and purpose!

Find strength within yourself, and your strength will express love and hope to others.

QUESTIONS AND INSIGHTS TO JOURNAL ABOUT STRENGTH

1. What is your superpower? How do you use it for good?

2. Do you have spiritual ears, eyes, nose, mouth, or touch? Ears that can hear God talk. Eyes that can see the Truth. A nose that can smell the goodness. A mouth that sings the praises of Spirit. A healing touch. If so, how do you use these powers and how do they work for you?

3. How patient are you? What are some ways that you can practice patience?

4. When someone feels differently about something than you do, can you still see them? Rather than push them away, can you invite them in? Can you appreciate them for who they are and for their honesty?

5. Have you ever taken the time to look into someone's eyes and say to them, "I see you?" Try practicing it with someone you trust. You may be surprised at how much closer you will feel to that special someone.

6. How can you become stronger and help others become stronger as well?

Resources
Read: *The Purpose Driven Life: What on Earth Am I Here For?* by Rick Warren.

Do you have any idea how splendid and magnificent you really are? There is no one else exactly like you in the world. There never has been and never will be. You are strong, invincible, and free.

CHAPTER SIX:
SPIRITUAL WISDOM

Personally, I believe my wisdom—such as it is—has grown through being willing to learn from my life experiences and not hiding from them or diminishing their importance to my growth. I've also found it helpful to continuously search for ways to grow and expand on all levels—physically (as in wholeness not in size), mentally, emotionally, and spiritually.

There are many great teachers among us and who have come before us from whom we can study and learn. It's important to choose your teachers wisely and go with your gut feelings when spending time with them or studying their work. Most of my greatest teachers have been family and friends. Sometimes they have taught me what to do and other times what not to do. Other teachers have appeared through readings, workshops, group interactions, schools, and people I have encountered in everyday settings like the grocery store. Keep your eyes and ears open in your search for teachers. Retain the good ones and release the rest!

Each one of us enters this world with a mission. The wise ones already know this. They have identified their mission and live it out every day of their lives.

The wisdom of our minds has many windows. When we look out of or into these windows, we need to be clear about what we are looking for and what we are seeking.

Make a commitment, an appointment with life. So often I hear people say, "I'll do that soon" or, when … "I feel better, my ship comes in, I'm more financially secure, I retire." Remember soon is not a time and some is not a number. So, stay accountable to yourself and do it now!

Thoughts are things that travel through space like cell phone waves to the people we are thinking about. Own your thoughts, feelings, and behavior. Think only positive, healthy, and joy-filled thoughts. This is not a burden. It is freeing and empowering! We have little or no control over others, but we do have total control over our own thoughts and actions. Let patience, love, and peace be your daily practice. May this practice guide your thoughts, words, and actions as it guided the shepherds many years ago.

As we travel through our days, we constantly meet ourselves in others. The negative we see in others is always a reflection back to ourselves. Be grateful for the lessons and continue onward. Don't be concerned about what others are saying or doing. Focus on what you are doing to live out your purpose. By observing you, others will follow and will also take up hope. Despite what is presented in physical reality, can you see everyone in their highest light—happy, whole, healthy, and full of vitality? This is who we really are, and deeply knowing this wisdom will help you and everyone around you.

Listen to the wisdom of Mother Earth as she sings and laughs with you. Live in the present moment and shine your light like the brightest star in the sky. We do not fall out of an airplane and into heaven. Instead, we grow in grace, wisdom, and understanding and find heaven right where we are.

When you feel stuck and are not sure of what you want, take a deep breath and search inside yourself. Know who you are and follow your own wisdom. The golden age is already here. Do you plan to join the negative herd, or will you learn to determine your own intentions and enjoy a most rewarding life? It's up to you! It is simple, but not easy!

Our thoughts create our lives. That's why your Truth is not someone else's Truth. What we resist, persists. What we fight, fights back. What you think, you link. Replace your negative thoughts with positive ones and watch your life become easier and more peaceful.

Our past is not who we are. It's not a part of our current physical reality. Let's honor and embrace our past and move on to be present in this time and place. See yourself and others in the highest light—happy, healthy, joyful, and whole. Allow wisdom and grace to be your guides everyday.

When we move one part of our body, it affects other parts of our body. When we make choices, it affects more than just ourselves. Be careful with your body and be wise with your choices. When combined together, what we think, eat, say, and believe create who we are. Be very thoughtful and conscientious about these activities.

Since you chose to buy a ticket to this life, make sure you don't watch only half of the show!

Today I choose to be a little more humble. "When pride comes, then comes disgrace, but with humility comes wisdom."—Proverbs 11:2.

All thoughts, ideas, and manifestations in our world have their inception in Spirit. Spirit is the Creator, and your mind is the builder. The flow comes from the Master's Mind to the human mind to expressions in the physical world. This is the natural flow of all that is. All things in our material world existed first in the spiritual world. Our minds are the creators and builders of our physical world. You already know what to do, so just be in the flow and do it! And be aware of what you think about all day long, as these thoughts are creating your world.

There is no right path to Spirit. Don't waste your time searching for it or working toward it. Spirit is already here, inside you, outside you, and all around you. Spend your time living in Spirit and communing with it.

If you are true to yourself and can see the beauty and good in yourself first, you will be able to be true to others and see the beauty and good in them, even in those you perceive as your enemies.

Fame and fortune will often take wings and fly away. Love, truth, and integrity remain forever. You may feel that you have gained the whole world, but still lose yourself if you don't understand why your soul entered this plane at this particular time and in this special place.

We can learn so much by watching the sunset and listening to beautiful music, the sound of laughter, or the song of a bird. Each has its own message, direct from the Creator.

Always remember: What you do today creates tomorrow's memories. Be careful about what you do today so you are making good memories for tomorrow.

QUESTIONS AND INSIGHTS TO JOURNAL ABOUT SPIRITUAL WISDOM

1. Have you identified your mission? If so, what is it and how are you living it out?

2. What does it mean to you to own your thoughts, words, and actions? Do you find this to be freeing?

3. What have you noticed in others recently, good or bad, that may be a reflection back to you? How do you respond when you recognize the mirror?

4. If you could meet yourself as a young child, what message would you share with your child-self? If you could project ten years into the future, what would you tell your present self? What do you want your life to look like ten years from now? What do you want your mind–body to become?

5. To schedule your days and accomplish your priorities, think about what one thing you can do today to help you be where you want to be in ten years.

6. Recall a recent vacation, retreat, or time away from your normal life, and reflect on what lessons you have learned during your time away.

7. Since your life is a printout of your subconscious mind, stop and ask yourself, "Where am I struggling?" Once you can identify your struggles, you can change your thoughts and change your life?

Resources
Read **https://www.theladders.com/ career-advice/10-important-life-lessons-we-are-often-taught-too-late**

Look into the mirror every day and say to yourself, "I am one of a kind. Yes, I am."

CHAPTER SEVEN:

DANCING WITH THE DIVINE

From a very young age, I knew there was something bigger than me that guided and protected me throughout my days and nights. This has always been a great comfort to me, and has allowed me to live my life fearlessly.

I love to travel and explore, and have traveled alone on road trips throughout the United States. While attending seminary, I walked the streets of New York City alone at night. My travel bug has taken me around the world, to places like Kenya and Russia. All of these experiences happened with excitement and awe and with little or no fear because of my faith in the Divine to protect and watch over me, no matter where I am or what I'm doing.

One thing I do first thing when I wake every morning is to thank the Divine for the gift of today and to make a list of what I am grateful for. It's a great way to start each new day and to remind me that I am never alone. Why not join me?

Spirit's peaceful way makes all things new. Pray every day for Spirit to help you remember who you really are and why you are here.

When you are facing a mountain to climb, imagine Spirit shrinking it right before your eyes. When you are met with confusion and life confounds you, trust the Divine to guide you through. If you're feeling overwhelmed and don't have enough time in your day, ask Spirit to control your calendar.

Spirit is life! Activity and movement are the results of the activity of Spirit. Just as movement or tension in one area of our body affects our whole body, so our thoughts, words, and actions affect not only ourselves but others as well. Invite Spirit to lead your thoughts, words, and actions upward and outward in service to your sisters and brothers. It is better to act in error than to not act at all.

What we call problems are simply illusions or mistakes of the mind. Since Spirit is everywhere, bring it into your problems and watch them dissolve. In the world of Spirit, problems don't exist. Only we can bring problems into physical reality. "You don't have a problem, you just think you do." (A Course In Miracles)

You are not what you have done, nor what has been done to you. You are limitless in Spirit. This is your true essence. We will only find the Divine in the present moment, so let's give up the past and the future. Spirit is alive in the here and now. When we are living from our Divine Nature, we can always begin again.

Live Confidently—Do not fear. For you are secure in love and peace. The presence of God is always within and all around you.

When we set our hopes on our own specific outcomes, we may be disappointed. When we accept that Spirit is working through us and remain open and receptive, we'll lead happier lives. Wait and watch expectantly and when you pray, always ask for "this or something better."

Everything in the material world comes from Spirit, from Divine Mind to our human mind to material expression. However, we do need to add some effort and energy to the process. It is our job to maintain balance within our hearts and minds so the outside world does not have a great effect on us. Remain firm in your happiness in spite of what is going on around you.

We all experience storms in our lives. The trick to weathering them with grace and ease is to turn them over to Spirit. When you are shaken by external experiences, remember that Spirit is always with you. Nothing can throw your Spirit off balance. When you want or need to make renovations and major changes in your life, start by asking the Divine to help you renovate your heart first. Don't go looking for or creating storms in your life. They will come soon enough. When they do come, stay in the center of the storm where all is peaceful and calm.

There is no need to internalize the external world. We are able to shift our attention and our thoughts to be happy and joyful, even in the worst of times. Keep your priorities straight!

Remember who you are! Spirit in a human body, only more perfect, powerful, and blessed than your human mind can ever imagine. We come into this world as spiritual beings. Our biggest and most difficult challenge is to learn how to become fully human. Now is the time to nurture, water, fertilize, and shine the sun on your Spirit so it may thrive and bloom in this beautiful garden of life. Invite Spirit to reside within you. There will be painful times of necessary pruning and also glorious times of beautiful blossoming.

Be patient and keep the faith. All necessary things will come to you, for everything comes from and belongs to the Divine. Life is an adventure! Breathe and remember that you are a spiritual being sent here to express the Divine through your daily life experiences. May your Spirit fly higher and brighter today than ever before.

If you want to know the Divine Sweet Spirit, give praise and glory while doing good unto others. Minister to others as well as to yourself. Set aside your own agenda today to help someone else. People are not looking for advice, nor do they want to be fixed or saved. They simply want to be seen and heard, so open your ears and be the witness.

If we live from the Divine within us, there is no need to try to be good, kind, or peaceful. One can just be, and the rest will take care of itself. When we breathe, we breathe the breath of Spirit. Everything we do, we do within Spirit. We are all the unique expression of the Divine.

Grace often shows up when we least expect it. Gifts of truth, justice, mercy, grace, and love come from the Divine. But when you need grace and it isn't showing up, don't be afraid to ask the Divine for help. And remember, you can only receive these gifts by living them and sharing them with others.

QUESTIONS AND INSIGHTS TO JOURNAL
ABOUT THE DIVINE

1. So, I've been pondering the difference between our soul and our spirit. Are they different or the same? Is one the inner and the other the outer? What are your thoughts?

2. Are you able to see beyond the physical world and allow Spirit to be your guide? Allow the physical to just fall into place. What does that look like for you?

3. Problems result from our belief that we are separate from Spirit and each other. Try exploring this illusion. Are you able to change your mind and release your problems?

4. What does Spirit want you to do and are you willing to obey? Have you met and do you interact with your spirit guides? We all have guides who are patiently waiting for us to ask them for help. When you meditate or are in your sacred and quiet place, ask your spirit guides to show you who they are and ask them for specific ways in which they can help you. Interact with them today and every day.

5. I am Divine. You are Divine. We are Divine. And so it is! How does this resonate with you? In what ways do you see yourself as Divine?

6. Are you able to just be? If you always need to be busy and in perpetual motion, what are some things that will help you to slow down and relax?

7. Can you imagine yourself face to face with Spirit? If so, try talking with Spirit about your concerns and your dreams. What would you like to say to or ask of Spirit?

8. Join me in sitting with the questions. What does Spirit want me to do, and am I willing to obey? After asking myself this question, my life has become quieter and my soul has become noisier.

9. What does freedom look like to you? If our Divine Nature is wholly free, can we ever really be imprisoned?

10. What are you doing right now to shine your light and bring joy to this world?

Resources
Watch on YouTube: https://www.youtube.com/watch?v=g0zU2EoRfMw
Dream Big by Denzel Washington

Everything truly important is invisible.
Only our hearts and Spirit can see the truth.
Spirit's got you!

CHAPTER EIGHT:

THE SWEETNESS OF SURRENDER

My journey to becoming an interfaith minister is one of my stories of personal surrender. All my life, I've known that I am more than my body and my mind, and as an adult, I came to realize that many others did not have this same understanding.

After becoming involved with the Unity Church, I began to explore and study spiritual teachings, particularly how different religions and faith traditions viewed and taught them. This led me to enroll in classes at Unity Village with my dear friend David and, eventually, these classes led me to become a Licensed Unity Teacher.

During this time, I proclaimed to myself and to others that I had no interest or calling to become ordained. I'm not really sure why I thought this way. Most likely it was from fear, the fear of surrendering to my true spiritual calling.

As a licensed teacher, I was soon asked to perform ceremonies in addition to teaching classes. When my great niece, Kayla, asked me to perform her wedding ceremony, the light bulbs began to go off and I seriously started to consider pursuing ordination. In Pennsylvania, the state requires that you be licensed or ordained to join couples in wedded bliss. After I performed the ceremony, I needed to have a friend pronounce my niece's vows and sign the marriage license.

This led me to search for a seminary that would support my rather free-spirited approach to spirituality. I explored Unity, Moravian, and Lutheran seminaries, and eventually attended an information session at

One Spirit in New York City. Here I found my spiritual home and spent two years on a life-changing journey to ordination.

And, I surrendered. I surrendered many of my false beliefs, not only about different religions and spiritual practices but also about the differences in people—race, color, sexual identity, backgrounds, and ancestors. It was a mind-expanding and spiritual awakening that I had never experienced before or since.

I often compare my life's journey to the seasons of the year. The seasons of life are very much the same as the seasons of Mother Nature.

Spring is beautiful and lush. Flowers are plentiful, trees are full of blooms, and the grass is bright green. Spring is a time for us to emerge from our winter's rest, be reborn, and bloom into a brand new version of ourselves.

Summer is hot and sultry. We become fully awake as we experience the Summer Solstice, the longest day of the year. Our Spirits are alive, refreshed, and energized. On long summer days, our Spirits yearn to be out, to feel alive, and to celebrate.

Autumn is a time to honor the harvest, the harvest of our intentions and efforts we set earlier in the year. The fall equinox brings us equal time, a twelve-hour day and a twelve-hour night. Fall is a time to clear out your internal space and create room for your winter hibernation.

Winter brings us shorter days and longer nights. As the dark triumphs over the light, we are invited to rest and reflect, to go within and experience the silence. Soon we will begin re-awakening and slowly building toward brighter days.

Let's surrender our attachment to things. Use the things of the world, and then release them. Only what comes from Spirit is everlasting. We need to die to our small self and be reborn to our higher self before we can truly live. Our false identity must surrender to our True Self.

There are only two realities in this world: love and fear. All emotions, actions, and reactions come from either love or fear. And, there are only two innate fears: the fear of falling and the fear of loud noises. Every other fear is learned, which means it can be unlearned. What a great reason for hope and for living your life with courage. Just for today, try surrendering your fears and seek out perfect love within you.

Be clear-minded—Release the past and envision the future, all while living in the present moment. It's possible, but not easy.

Surrender—We have to live life to its fullest before we can surrender. It's an ongoing process, not a one-and-done thing. With faith and understanding, joyously let go.

Are you asleep or awake? —Understanding others, the world around us, and the universe only comes about through truly understanding ourselves. On a spiritual level, we are always going to sleep and waking up. All we can do is study, experience, work through our need for attachment, and continually search for peace and understanding. Be conscious and awake, and choose what you pay attention to. Be aware of how you construct meaning from your experiences. If you don't, you may be out of luck!

The Paradox—As soon as you learn to give it all up, you can have it all. The sooner you release something, the quicker it will return to you. The moment you no longer want something, you will have more of it than you ever dreamed possible. Join me in releasing the past. Transform it or find a way to throw it away. Continuously clear out the stuff you no longer need—physically, emotionally, and spiritually. Reduce or eliminate schedules, inboxes, paperwork, clutter, errands, finances, pantry items, and the never-ending to-do lists. The past is over. Let's move on to better things together. Make way for the new!

Our lives are like plays or stories. Characters come and go—some are good and some are bad, but all of them are necessary. Embrace them all and move on to your next act.

The world and many people in it are unstable. We live in an ever-changing world. Nothing stands still! Everything either grows or deteriorates. Take what is growing into each new day and leave the rest behind. Transcend the world. Don't give it so much significance, and your life will be so much simpler.

Do you spend your days busily waiting for the right time to do something in your life? Are you waiting for the right person, job, place, opportunity, or life situation to show up? Rather than waiting for a specific outcome or moment, try just living your life and watching expectantly. This will help bring new adventures into your life and will lessen the possibility of being disappointed.

QUESTIONS AND INSIGHTS TO JOURNAL ABOUT SURRENDER

1. Do you look forward to spring as a time of renewal and rebirth in your life?

1. How are you doing with surrendering your attachment to things?

2. Do you agree that the only two emotions and responses in physical reality are love and fear? If not, what else do you think comes into play with your emotions and reactions?

3. Just for one hour, watch your thoughts and allow them to flow freely. Don't accept or reject them, just observe them. Reflect on some of your thoughts. What was this experience like? What did you learn?

4. Are you able to observe your thoughts, but not necessarily accept them as true? Our minds can be tricky, wanting us to believe that all of our thoughts are true and have meaning. Trust me. They aren't and they don't!

5. Can you find the place inside yourself where there is no fear, only love? Can you be quiet enough so that you aren't contributing to the chaos of the physical world?

Resources
Watch This: https://pemachodronfoundation.org/videos/fear-and-fearlessness/

"No one and no thing is against you."
—Gary Simmons

CHAPTER NINE:
PEACE BEGINS WITH ME

As I mentioned previously, I experience very little fear in my life. For this reason, I also experience a high level of peace. This has been my personal experience since I was a very young child. It has supported me in being adventurous on many different levels, including traveling outside my comfort zone in both my emotional/mental and physical worlds.

From my last count, I have traveled to forty countries and all but four states in the United States. My travels have expanded not only my outer world but my inner world as well, as I meet and interact with people who are very different from me in culture, living environments, and religious affiliations. One of the most important things I have learned in all of my travels is that although people appear different from me on a surface level, almost everyone desires many of the same things that I do: family, friends, love, and peace!

I realize that physical travel is not something everyone can experience or enjoys. If this is true for you, there are many other ways to travel—through books, movies, podcasts, videos, and conversations with other people who have traveled. The important thing is to always ask questions and be curious, to always be learning and exploring our world and beyond, as much as is humanly possible for you.

No matter what's going on around us, we can find peace in our hearts through prayer and meditation. Find someplace today that represents peace for you and spend time there. The secret to life is finding the peace of Spirit in your heart and in your life. Just for this minute, this hour, this day, plan to reside in a place of perfect peace. Cast out fear and find the divine source of love and peace inside you.

Enjoy the present moment. Don't allow your past to define you and don't worry about the future. Allow your life to be filled with so much love that each day brings you greater joy and more beauty. Allow love to rule your life. Don't allow worry to enter your physical being, as it will not improve your conditions. Know that you're equipped to meet the needs of whatever challenges come your way. I know, it's easier said than done, but let's just try.

When there is no peace in our hearts, we cannot pray for, create, or practice peace. Practice peace within yourself and watch it manifest in your relationships with others. Create peace in your own life, heart, and soul, and take that out into the world. Be for something—peace, joy, love, hope. Never be against anything! If you can see the world through the eyes of peace and love, the whole world will reflect back to you as peaceful and loving. Try blessing the world with a peaceful heart.

We live our lives from within, from the inside out. Know who you are, know in whom and in what you believe, and then apply it to your relationships and your daily life.

Relax and allow Spirit to get its arms around you. Be awake, alert, aware, present, and more peaceful in your own life. Live life quietly and peacefully in the present moment, see the beauty all around you and allow the future to unfold as it will. Allow your thoughts to be more constructive, more patient, more loving, more peaceful, and more humble. Release resentments and don't allow yourself to get so mad over little things. Keep the peace!

The current physical reality may be spotlighting faults and failures in ourselves and others. Let us release finding fault in others and in ourselves. Let's work on improving ourselves and allow others to work on improving themselves. May peace and mercy guide our words and activities. This is the way to peace and hope.

The origins of peace and joy lie in your very own home. Home Sweet Home! Find and practice peace and joy in your home, and then you and your loved ones can take it out into the world.

May peace find a resting place in your heart today. May it flow into your daily activities and the minds and hearts of those around you. Don't be anxious about anything. The peace and guidance of prayer are always available to us in the silence and through the grace and presence of Spirit. In every situation, pray with gratitude and present your requests to Spirit. Only then will you find peace beyond all understanding.

When you start with peace and harmony within yourself, you will also begin to find it in your relationships at home, at work, and all around you. Peace and harmony bring beauty to all things and all circumstances. Once you find it within yourself, all good things will come to you. If you desire more peace and harmony, try volunteering to be of service to others. Through service to others, the Spirit of Truth will deepen within you and you will know peace, harmony, and joy. Happy and harmonious homes will deliver the soul of our nation and our world from the spoilers.

Light always dissolves darkness. Love always replaces hate. Spirit always cancels problems. Wait patiently. Do not wander in the darkness looking for the light. The light is already there, right in the heart of the darkness. Be the light. Be Peace!

QUESTIONS AND INSIGHTS TO JOURNAL ABOUT PEACE

1. Are you feeling peaceful today? If not, how can you change your thoughts to peaceful ones?

2. How can you deepen the all-important qualities of peace and harmony?

3. Do you sometimes see yourself as a separate being from other living beings and the world around you? If so, how can you work on dispelling this illusion of separation to gain more internal peace?

4. How do you refresh your Spirit? When, where, and how often do you meditate and/or pray? How can you find ways to increase and deepen these practices?

5. Do you have a ritual that helps you find peace? If not, create one. Remember, "Peace be Still!"

6. When you are feeling out of sorts, try repeating this Buddhist blessing: "May you be filled with loving-kindness. May you be safe from inner and outer dangers. May you be well in body and mind. May you be at ease and happy."

7. Is your home a place where angels desire to visit and want to be your guest? If not, what can you do to create a place where angels come to visit?

Resources
Try finding peace through coloring:
Peace and Love: Adult Coloring Book by Blush Design
Read: *The Boundary Boss* by Terri Cole

"We are all just walking each other home."
Ram Dass

CHAPTER TEN:
LOVE EVERYONE AND EVERYTHING

As I have aged and matured, my understanding and pursuit of love have moved from the romantic, storybook concept of typical human love relationships to the pursuit of a different form of love—that of loving everyone and everything that comes into my life.

Of course this is not easy, and it comes with many challenges and opportunities to do my work. For example, when someone comes into my life who is difficult for me to love, or a situation arises that appears on the surface to be negative, how do I turn these situations around so that I can feel and send love to that person or that situation?

Here are several ways that that work for me. Still not easy, but certainly worth the time and effort as, in the long run, life becomes easier when it is filled with more love:

I take time every day to refresh my Spirit. I find that room with a view in my inner sanctuary and go there to find peace and serenity. Our hearts are designed for perfect love, and our minds are created for total peace. Remember this as you move through your days. Like all things, love takes practice. Love is a decision. Love builds bridges. Love casts out fear. There is only Love!

It is possible to overcome all obstacles with Love. Be kind, cheerful, and encouraging. This will help not only those around you but yourself even more. It's our job as light workers to maintain peace in our hearts so the world does not have a great effect on us. Focus on the good, no matter what is going on around you.

As we judge others, so too shall we be judged. Whatever we do unto others, we also do onto ourselves and onto Spirit. That's why it's so important to replace judgment with love. Be a love-finder rather than a faultfinder, and you will be filled with joy. Our only real enemy is fear. It can destroy our mental intelligence and our emotional balance. Fear can only be overcome by love. First, love yourself, and then spread that love to others.

Love life fully so that you can live in a way that will make your efforts, mind, soul, and body flourish. Allow your Divinity to be in full bloom, don't hide it away! Let your light shine in the lives of those you meet every day. Try to not get weary, but be joyous in service, bringing hope and love into the lives of others. Just as you feed your physical body with food and your mind with knowledge, feed your Spirit with a regular diet of soul vitamins.

Become a vessel of love and you will be wrapped up and protected in the loving arms of Spirit. Be the way of love! If we wish to receive love, we must be loving. Love is the key to everything. Without love, there is nothing. Once we are able to love everything the world contains—our fellow travelers, creatures and inanimates, the visible and invisible—we will know the Oneness and everything will become a miracle. Be gentle with yourself and with others. Kind words will soften anger, bring joy, and will make for a brighter day for you and everyone around you. Live and create from your heart with ease and peace. You are safe in the arms of the Universe. Be kind and gentle.

Divine Love is the most desired love of all. Divine love is joyous. It can give and just be what it is. Don't allow your ego to distract you from being Divine Love. Love is giving and growing. Love is selfless, enduring, and understanding, and it is the creator of opportunities, even in times of adversity.

Do the best with what you have. Take care of yourself, both on the inside and the outside. Keep your spirit, mind, and body temple beautiful, and you will love yourself more and more. Ask the Holy Spirit to inspect you and wash you clean. A clean heart is a joyful heart.

The only problem today in our country and the world is the illusion of separation. Since we are all one, love your neighbors, for they are a reflection of you. Make your own path straight, don't worry about the paths of others, and you will find peace and hope. We have no power to straighten another's path. We can only live by example. But you can shine your light so brightly that it lights the path for others to find their way.

We come into this world as little bundles of love and joy. It's our natural state. Our task as adults is to find unconditional love by locating and removing all obstacles we have built within ourselves against love.

Just for today, let's love each other. If you are grateful to be alive, then be patient with your neighbors. Show love and send blessings to everyone. Become a center of love, and everything else will fall into place. See no strangers. Be curious about your opponents and tend to their wounds. Try replacing fear with curiosity. At the same time, don't hover. Release those you love into the care of Spirit.

Love can begin with a simple smile. From there, it grows into tender looks that become a habit and blossom into endless forgiveness. Create love, and you will bring joy, happiness, and hope to the world. Stay in the present moment, and you will find greater contentment. Make love, not war!

Love, love, love is everywhere. Whenever you're ready, you can tap into it. Plant seeds of love today and every day, fertilize them with hope, water with resolve, and add some sunny smiles. Grace, mercy, friendship, and love bloom, even in our material world. They become flowers of joy, happiness, peace, and understanding, making our journey on earth worthwhile. Love is the one thing that unites us all. It can inspire, encourage, and lighten hearts everywhere.

This is one of my favorite prayers: *May we all be safe. May we all give and receive love. May we all have everything we need. May we all pray for the highest good of every little thing.*

Stay alert and awake. Love Spirit, love yourself, and love your neighbor. What else is there? In every moment, Spirit responds to us with love, nothing but love. Today, plan to respond to everyone with love and allow love to prepare your way. Perfect love! The only place to find it is within Spirit. Stay close and in tune with the Holy Spirit. It knows just what you need. Stay humble and, with Spirit's help, watch yourself grow into a more beautiful human being each and every day. Receive and rest in the perfect love of Spirit.

Happiness is knowing real love, being in touch with it, and expressing it in your daily life. When we are in touch with our Creator and are in a space of love, hope, and joy, we lose sight of ourselves. This is when we experience true happiness. Love is invisible, and it cannot be seen or measured. Yet, it is so powerful that it can bring more joy into our lives than all the material things of the world.

We have the freedom to choose our own actions—free will—and with that comes consequences. Look for the love in the consequences. Own your own story, don't hide from it! We all need to explore the darkness in order to find the light. Everyone has a story that will break your heart and bring you to your knees, so be gentle and kind with everyone you meet.

Heart Space—It's a short trip from your head to your heart (about eighteen inches). It's an even shorter trip from your physical heart to your spiritual heart. Try both trips today, and enjoy the journey.

Love your neighbor as yourself is an age-old saying, but who is your neighbor? Is it the one who lives next door or the one who lives on the other side of the world? Is it the person who is most like you and thinks like you, or is it the person who is different from you? I say both. Try loving both. Recognize the courage and resolve of all people to live freely and authentically. Affirm your obligation to uphold the dignity of all people.

Love good, love honor, love patience! Divine Love brings wisdom and healing, and extends far beyond the grave. Spiritual laws are eternal and unchangeable. Love is law. Love is Spirit. Truth is law. Truth is Spirit. Love and Truth are eternal, and they will set you free!

Remember to seek comfort from your own inner Spirit. It will never come from the outer world. Contentment, peace, love, beauty, and joy all come from within and allow us to grow and positively express ourselves in this world. I wish for you a comfortable day, no matter what is going on around you. It's a crazy world around us right now, and we are all grieving everyday losses. But we can always find comfort in the arms of the Divine.

I'm sending you hugs (virtual, of course) for comfort. Take them and internalize them. Now send them on to others who need hugs of comfort right now. Be kind and comforting to one another. We're all going in the same direction, and are only one step away from "home".

Attend to the ear of your heart. Listen closely and lovingly to everybody and everything today, including yourself. Remember to listen to that still, small voice within you that teaches you how to love and warns you about all dangers. It will protect you from missteps and unnecessary suffering.

Can you feel and sometimes even see the Dance of Energy and Love inside you and all around you? Be sure to join in the dance!

Be true to yourself. Hold tight to your own beliefs and principles. Do something every day to manifest love for yourself, and then reflect that love out to others.

Wake up and remember who you are. Keep your face toward the light and allow your heart to sing. There is joy in knowing that you are one with all, including your Creator, who has the power to meet all of your needs. Always direct everything—your thoughts, hopes, dreams, desires, actions—toward the Light.

At day's end, when you count your blessings, remember anyone who you may have held outside your heart. Invite them back in before you go to sleep.

Join me in seeing a world where everyone lives in love, peace, and harmony; speaks with kindness and encouragement to others; and feels safe and loved at all times.

It's our job as humans to remain balanced within our hearts, focused on happiness. Then the world will not have much effect on us, no matter what is going on around us. Stay awake and nudge others awake as well. Put your power of imagination to its highest and best use for all beings everywhere.

QUESTIONS AND INSIGHTS TO JOURNAL ABOUT LOVE

1. Spirit is not loving. Spirit is Love! How can you be like that? How can you be not just loving, but love itself?

2. Do you truly love yourself? It's impossible to love the Divine and your neighbors if you don't love yourself first.

3. Take time today to perform a self-evaluation of your heart. A joyful heart will overflow with love and hope.

4. What does the phrase "ear of the heart" mean to you? How can you listen more carefully to this ear?

5. What does it mean to you to love outrageously? List some ways that you believe you can do this.

6. Write a love letter to yourself. Express your current joy in yourself and the joy you anticipate coming to you.

7. How much time did you invest last month in what you say is important to you? Do you spend the majority of your time with the people and projects that you love?

Resources
Listen to: Love, Serve, and Remember sung by John Austin

Love rules all!

CHAPTER ELEVEN:

EXPERIENCING GRIEF AND LOSS

Like everyone else, I have experienced many losses in my life, which have allowed me to experience and live through the grieving process.

Most recently, I lost my 100-year-old mother, who was one of the most loving and peaceful people I have ever known. Although I am very grateful to have had her in my life for such a long time, losing her was very traumatic.

While she was actively dying over a period of weeks, I often felt very alone as the people around me talked about how they planned to care for her and where she might live when she came home.

My mother and I both knew and accepted the fact that she was dying and had several opportunities to talk about this reality before she made her transition. She had a deep faith in God, and did not appear to be afraid of the mystery of where she was moving next. We both would have preferred that her dying process would have been less physically painful, but that part of the process also remains a mystery to me.

Although I miss her physical presence, it is much simpler now for me to communicate with her without the need for spoken words or devices. My mother is always just a thought away from me.

Even when we are alive, our loved ones are often out of sight but not out of mind. In death, loved ones are simply waiting for us to acknowledge them just around the corner.

Sometimes we run or hide from pain, believing that we cannot bear it. But we have already felt the pain. What we haven't done is allow ourselves to feel who we are beyond the pain. Do what works for you in your grieving process. Don't be concerned about what people tell you that you should do. Trust yourself, and do what works for you.

Grief is whatever you think and feel inside about the death of someone or the loss of something. The unexpected thoughts and behaviors you are experiencing because of a loss are part of your grief.

Grief is much more than just sadness. It is often a combination of feelings such as shock, confusion, anxiety, anger, regret, and sadness. The mixture of feelings can change from minute to minute, or from day to day.

Your grief will always be unique and will depend upon your relationship with the person who died or the situation surrounding your loss. The stronger your attachment to the person or the situation, the more difficult your grief journey will be. It only makes sense that the closer you felt to the person or situation, the more torn apart you will feel after your loss.

Ambivalent relationships can also cause complicated grief. You may feel a strong sense of unfinished business, such as things you wanted to say but never did, or conflicts you wanted to resolve but didn't.

It's okay to be happy or sad. It's okay to spend time alone or with family. Saying no is okay too. It doesn't matter how long ago the loss was, allow yourself to feel the grief and the pain. If it feels right, try saying yes to offers of help from others and allow people to support you.

Grief and loss bring about unexpected emotions, ranging from anger to sadness to emptiness to unexpected joy. Be open to all of these emotions and flow with them. And be kind and generous toward those around you who are also grieving.

Healing of the mind, body, or spirit comes thru the grace of the Divine. Ask for what you need and be persistent. Healing will come. Not in your time, but in Spirit's time. When you send healing prayers to others, you will also be healing yourself. In fact, you will be sending a little healing to the whole world. Keep an attitude of expectation and hope for the good. Believe in the healing power of positivity and love. Remain sweet!

It's a strange time that we live in, and we all grieve losses, even small everyday ones. But you can always find comfort in the arms of the Divine.

Death is real, while life is fleeting. Only Spirit lives eternally as a part of the Creative Energy. Enjoy your life, while at the same time looking forward to becoming a member of the Eternal Force.

While remembering loved ones who have passed through the veil, I pray and hold them in my consciousness. I believe they are often listening for our voices to speak to them.

QUESTIONS AND INSIGHTS TO JOURNAL ABOUT GRIEF AND LOST

1. Take time to describe a recent loss that you are grieving and the emotions that you are feeling around this loss.

2. What helps you when you are grieving? What kind of self-care do you need?

3. Identify a friend or kindred spirit who will support you on your journey. Reach out to that person and be willing to accept their support.

4. What does it mean to you to "die while you are alive?" Have you been able to experience anything like this? If so, try describing it in writing.

5. Here's a great question to answer: Before I die, I want to (fill in the blank). (Thank you, Barbara Becker, for this question.)

Resources
Read: *Heartwood, The Art of Living With The End in Mind,* by Barbara Becker
Explore Dr. Alan Wolfelt's website: www.centerforloss.com

> "Die while you are alive and be absolutely dead.
> Then do whatever you want—it's all good."
> —Zen Master Bunan

CHAPTER TWELVE:

LIVING FROM GRATITUDE

Life is hard. Since the beginning of humankind's arrival in this world, life has always been hard. Personally, my faith and willingness to dance with the Divine has made my life simpler and easier.

For the first several decades of my life, it was much harder than it has been for the last several decades. In my mid-thirties, I found and became involved with a group of women and men led by a woman named Jo Wimmer (thank you, Jo, for bringing us together) who were interested in progressing and evolving into better human beings.

We eventually formed a Master Mind Group and met every week for many years. We read and discussed the motivational books available at the time, and went on road trips to see many of the people who wrote these books. We saw Deepak Chopra, Bernie Segal, Louise Hay, and our all-time favorite, Wayne Dyer.

This was definitely the turning point in my life to moving from being self-involved and outwardly motivated to realizing that my life was so much richer and rewarding when I focused on my inner journey and on being of service to others. I finally became aware of the fact that my life was much more important and greater than I had ever imagined.

If you aren't already involved in a similar group, I strongly recommend that you search out and find one. Your life will become not only richer and more rewarding but easier as well.

Much of what our group studied had to do with being grateful just for being alive, just for being given this gift of life and all that comes with it, the good, the bad, and the ugly. We focused on being grateful for each other and grateful for every single thing that appears in our life.

Give thanks to Spirit for being alive and raise your voice in thanksgiving for those who add to the love and joy in your life. Keep your heart singing. Be joyful in service. Be happy with yourself, with others, and in new beginnings. Good vibrates on and on and never ends. So, do good things, say good things, and think good thoughts. Rejoice and be glad in it! It's a new day!

Everyone is asked to be of service, but not sacrifice. One simple act of service is to simply share your love—maybe only in your mind's eye—with everyone you encounter throughout your day. Grace comes abundantly to those who serve.

Try stretching yourself as you go through your days. Focus on what you agree with. Don't condemn or repeat anything that might be harmful to anyone. Be extravagant with your money, your time, your listening ear, and your kindness. Then be prepared to have a lovely day.

Being grateful makes you happier! It increases your positive emotions and helps you become more optimistic and giving. If you are grateful to be alive, then be patient with your fellow travelers. Show love and send blessings to everyone. As we travel through our days, we see ourselves in others. The negative we see in others is only our own reflection. Be grateful for the lessons and travel onward. Can you just be grateful for the breath that you breathe?

Hidden things—Search for the joy in hidden things. Enjoy the simple things in life: Watching the catbirds on the suet feeder, eating cupcakes baked by our neighbor's granddaughter, long phone calls with loved ones, daily walks with the dogs. Try watching the wonders of nature in your own little corner of the world, like birds fluttering and flowers showing off while butterflies feed on their nectar. Life can be simple and still very good.

Be optimistic! Rather than being against anything or anyone, be for something—kindness, healthiness, cheerfulness, peace, joy, gladness, healing, and hope. This will not only help you but it will help others around you as well. Be joyful in the way you live, in your relationships, and in your daily activities. Remember, joy and happiness create more joy and happiness.

Use your gifts for good, and more good will come to you. In order to honor your Creator, do the best with what you have and with what has been given to you. There is always enough in this world, not only for you but also for everyone. Lose yourself in the good, and prosperity and abundance will be yours for the asking.

Are you sleepwalking through life? What will it take for you to become fully awake and alive? Find what's sacred to you and follow it!

My Motto: When someone does something nice for you, just say, "Thank you." There is no need to argue with them or tell them they really shouldn't have. If someone compliments you, wants to buy you lunch, or gives you a gift, the most loving response is a heartfelt thank you. With this practice, both the giver and the receiver will receive a gift.

Love with your whole heart, be ever curious, give thanks continuously, and be grateful for all of your gifts. Don't take your blessings for granted. Watch where you place your attention, and remember to place it on the miracles that are all around you. Some days, I'm grateful for the simple things in life: a lovely sunset, lunch in the garden, ice cream for dinner, and for the very air that I breathe.

Each of us has our own purpose, which is actually an obligation, to act out in this lifetime. Know what your obligation is, act it out, and you will be a blessing for others.

Human connection is simply the exchange of positive energy between two people. Feeling understood and connected has the power to inspire change and build trust. Be the channel through which others may find grace, peace, harmony, and joy. Be of service to humankind by helping others find the Kingdom of Heaven right here on earth. When you meet someone for the first time and you feel like you've known them forever, they are most likely someone you knew in a past life. Go out and connect today!

Active listening is a deep form of respect. It's what people want more than anything else: to be truly heard. Do you truly listen when others are speaking?

QUESTIONS AND INSIGHTS TO JOURNAL ABOUT GRATITUDE

1. What hidden things bring you joy? Why do you consider these things to be hidden?

2. Since being grateful can actually make you happier, list some things that you are grateful for right now. Include some simple things like ice cream, sunsets, or pretty flowers.

3. Every morning, I list at least three things that I am grateful for while I am journaling. Find a time and place where you can do the same. It doesn't matter what time of the day or night. Just do it every day.

4. What is your gift to the world? Take time to identify and know your gift, and then allow your life to be an example of that gift. Always remember that you are a blessing to the world.

5. Reflect on ways that you can become a better receiver of gifts. Think about how you responded to people who have gifted you in the past and how you might respond differently in the future.

6. Gratitude doesn't always need to be acknowledged out loud. Try doing it silently with everyone who crosses your path and in the silence of your heart–mind.

7. Make a list of what brings you inexpressible joy and makes you smile. Make a gratitude "smile" list, and read it when you are having a bad day.

8. Since gratitude is a practice, take time today to call someone you love just to say, "I'm grateful for you in my life."

9. Count your blessings one by one and then make a list of at least ten blessings you have in your life. Share at least one of these blessings everyday with the rest of the world.

10. Share a smile, a cheery greeting, or a joyful wave with everyone you see today. In your mind's eye, wash the feet of every person you interact with. Then watch the love flow.

11. What in your life is preventing you from being grateful right now?

Resources
Check out Staci Danford on gratitude www.thegratefulbrain.com

May you be the type of person that everyone is happy to see you arrive and sad to see you go.

CHAPTER THIRTEEN:
THE GIFT OF MEDITATION AND PRAYER

I wrote this in 2012 for a class on meditation I led at Unity Village while studying to become a Licensed Unity Teacher:

"With the latest scientific studies proving that regular meditation makes you happier and healthier, we are already starting to see mainstream doctors prescribe meditation, relaxation, and breathing practices along with prescription drugs, and more psychiatrists dispensing meditation first before more potentially harmful medication. This includes the offering of meditation classes in hospitals and clinics, and the start of health insurance reimbursement for alternative and holistic methods."

"Taking this a step further, it won't be long before we start seeing meditation classes in public schools, meditation breaks instead of coffee breaks in the workplace, and meditation meetings beside prayer meetings in the halls of Congress. And, won't that be a great improvement over what is currently happening!"

Many of the things that I wrote about more than ten years ago are already taking place or are being discussed and in the planning stages. Many of my local schools have introduced meditation and relaxation practices into their classrooms, with teachers trained in how to carry out these techniques.

Just think about all of the great prophets who spent vast amounts of time alone, in silence, praying and meditating. For example:

Buddha sat under the Bodhi Tree and reached enlightenment (bodhi) after meditating beneath the tree for forty-nine days.

Jesus went off alone in the Judaean Desert and fasted for forty days and forty nights.

Muhammad was meditating in a cave on Mount Hira when he saw the Angel Jibril.

You might find it helpful to follow their example by taking time to savor Spirit everyday. Feed your Spirit and your mind with positive thoughts and feelings. Create a daily time and place where you can be silent and alone with your thoughts. Attend spiritual and meditation retreats as often as possible. Read, write, and converse with like-minded travelers about your spiritual journey. These endeavors will help to ensure that you are spiritually fed.

Remember, the quiet, alert, and thoughtful mind easily aligns with Spirit, not the uneasy, preoccupied, and busy mind. You are the eyes, ears, voice, hands, feet, and heart of the Creator. Walk softly on this earth and be gentle.

Pay attention to and search the paths of your interior movements. Eventually they will show up in your external world. Listen for and pay close attention to the inner voice of silence. Our only true guidance comes from within.

When you are in the middle of a storm, stay safe and warm. Take advantage of this time to pray and meditate.

Bite your tongue! If it is impossible to say nice things about a person, keep silent, even though what you want to say may be true.

To change anything, you must always start with yourself first. Set your intentions for your day first thing every morning. Know that you will create all that you need in spite of what's going on around you. Your thoughts and words have power.

Despite what we may believe, our thoughts are not our reality. Until they are acted upon, they are only imaginings and perceptions. Only we can give meaning and importance to them. Or not! We create our thoughts and words, label them, and then believe they are real. Trust me, they aren't! Watch your thoughts and your words closely and withhold your attention from anything that doesn't feel right. Words of wisdom from my sister: "If it hurts, don't do it!"

Prayer is not an option, it is a necessity. I have an ongoing conversation with Spirit. Prayer or entering into the silence regularly happens when it becomes a part of our daily routine. Pray in the form of an affirmation to your inner self and there you will find grace and peace.

When I visited Sarajevo, Bosnia, and I heard the call to prayer, I immediately dropped into my heart. Where do you go when you are called to pray? Do you have a favorite place to relax, pray, or meditate? Envision that kind of place internally and carry it with you everywhere.

The God of big ears—My dear friend Donna writes about praying to the God with big ears. Our prayers are not always answered in the way we want, but they are always answered.

Practice the pause! This is a very simple spiritual practice. When in doubt, speak up, speak your truth, but be kind. Take a deep breath and pause before you speak, press send, or post. When angry, pause. When tired, pause. When stressed, pause. When confused, pause. And when you are in that time of pause, pray.

QUESTIONS AND INSIGHTS TO JOURNAL ABOUT MEDITATION AND PRAYER

1. What is the difference between prayer and meditation? For me, prayer is communicating with Spirit and meditation is being still in body, mind, and heart and listening. What about you?

2. How do you pray? What does your prayer life look like? Are you satisfied with it, or are there ways you would like to improve upon it?

3. Describe your favorite place to pray and/or meditate. Can you envision it internally and carry it with you wherever you go?

4. Remove yourself from the cares of the world for a short time everyday. As often as you can, get close to nature and observe the birds, trees, flowers, and bees and observe how they are just being who they are and not trying to be something else.

5. What supports your meditation practice? Do you have special music, a mantra, silence, a special place, chanting, the sound of the ocean, the wind, or the rain that helps connect your heart with the heart of Spirit? Meditate as often as you can!

6. Where do you focus your attention? Is it on the negative or is it on the good all around you? Try taking this thought into meditation and see where it takes you.

7. Do you believe your thoughts and imaginings have meaning? Write about whether they do or don't.

8. Check in with yourself daily and write about your thoughts and feelings. This one small thing will make your life so much more fulfilling.

Resources
Check this out: The Music of James Anthony Walker -
https://www.theartofjim.com/

Let's keep our tender world in our prayers and good wishes every day.

CHAPTER FOURTEEN:

LESSONS LEARNED AT THE BEACH

It seems appropriate for the last chapter in my book to be about lessons from the beach, as this is where I found the time and motivation to take the writings from my journal and social media postings and transform them into a book format.

It's also interesting to me how my soul is drawn to the beach while my body reacts so negatively to the sun and the sand. I have a very fair complexion, with freckles, sensitive skin, and white hair, which was strawberry blonde when I was young. The first time I entered the office of a dermatologist to have a growth removed, the doctor said, "Oh my, red hair and freckles. We're in trouble and we'll be seeing a lot of each other."

My compromise between my body's discomfort and my soul's longing is to rent a place with a direct view of the beach and ocean where I can feed my soul as I enjoy the view and the sound of the waves without getting sunburned or skin rashes. An early morning or late day walk on the beach work perfectly for me, and the dogs don't care what time of the day we take our walks.

The main lesson I have learned from this experience is how we can respond to the yearning of our souls while still caring for our physical bodies. There's always a way to compromise.

Walk into the wind when you start walking on the beach, so that when you turn around the wind will help to blow you back home.

When it's windy and cool but you don't want to leave the beach, turn your chair around until you face the sun. If it's too cool and windy to sit on the beach, you can always walk on it. Plus, the dogs will be happy to join you.

When you are building anything, like the most difficult puzzle ever, don't give up! Keep at it until it's completed, even if it takes you all week!

If you wake up early, you will be rewarded with a beautiful sunrise over the ocean from right outside your bedroom window.

The ocean teaches us patience, serenity, faith, openness, simplicity, solitude, and rhythm. There are always more beaches to explore, more waves to watch, and more shells to find.

Each cycle of the tide is viable, each cycle of the wave is viable, and each cycle of your life is viable.

While waiting for your gifts from the Sea of Spirit, be open and receptive, as the beach is to the ocean.

Give me coffee to change the things I can, and the beach to accept the things I can't.

QUESTIONS AND INSIGHTS TO JOURNAL ON LESSONS FROM THE BEACH

1. What calls to your heart, the beach, forest, lakes, or streams?

2. When was your last trip to the beach? Write about your experience.

3. What gifts have you received from the beach or the ocean?

4. Can you be out in the sun, or are you more like me and need to avoid the sun and cover up? How does that make you feel?

5. How has each cycle of your life been viable, just like each cycle of the tide and waves are viable?

6. When you are working on something difficult, can you stick to it until it's completed, even if it's challenging and taking you a long time? Why or why not?

Resources
Read: *Gift From The Sea* by Anne Morrow Lindbergh

"Be in the world, but not of the world."
—Wayne Dyer

ACKNOWLEDGMENTS

Throughout my life, I have had many spiritual teachers and guides, and I'd like to thank a few of them here.

My three gurus, who have been instrumental in bringing this book to fruition:

Ram Dass—The first and foremost person who has influenced my spiritual journey.

Eckhart Tolle—Since reading his book, *The Power of Now*, I have been a follower and student of his.

Wayne Dyer—The most lovable, and the only one of the three I have actually met in person. Rather than have him autograph the book I had just purchased, I asked and received a hug from him instead. Thank you, Wayne!

My spiritual teachers:

Myrtle Fillmore (Unity co-founder and my role model), Edgar Cayce, Pema Chodron, Reverend Diane Berke (One Spirit), Helen Schucman (author of *A Course in Miracles*), Tom Thorpe (Unity Village), and Tony Burroughs (Intenders of the Highest Good).

I have way too many friends and family (aren't I blessed?) to list individually, but you know who you are and that I love you and always hold you in my heart

ADDITIONAL RESOURCES

BOOKS:

A Course In Miracles (ACIM) (1996), Foundation For Inner Peace, Mill Valley, CA

Brown, Brene' (2022), *The Gifts of Imperfection: 10th Anniversary Edition*, Hazelden Publishing, Center City, MN

Burroughs, Tony (2008) *The Code, 10 Intentions for a Better World*, Red Wheel/Weiser, LLC, San Francisco, CA

Chodron, Pema (1996) *Awakening Loving-Kindness*, Shambhala Publications, Inc., Boston, MA

Chopra, Deepak (2008) *The Third Jesus, The Christ We Cannot Ignore*, Harmony Books, New York

Cole, Terri (2021) *Boundary Boss, The Essential Guide to Talk True, Be Seen, and (Finally) Live Free*, Sounds True

Dass, Ram (2000) *Still Here, Embracing Aging, Changing, and Dying*, Riverhead Books, New York

Dyer, Dr. Wayne W. (2008) *Change Your Thoughts – Change Your Life: Living the Wisdom of the Tao*, Hay House Inc. Carlsbad, CA

Fillmore, Myrtle (2007) *How to Let God Help You*, Unity House, Unity Village, MO

Lindbergh, Anne Morrow (2002) *Wisdom From Gift From The Sea*, Peter Pauper Press Inc., White Plains, NY

The Essential Rumi, Translations by Coleman Barks, (2004) HarpersCollins Publishers, New York, NY

Tolle, Eckhart (2005) *A New Earth Awakening to Your Life's Purpose*, Penguin Group, New York, NY

Weiss, Brian L., M.D. (1988), *Many Lives, Many Masters*, Simon & Schuster, Inc., New York, NY

ONLINE RESOURCES:

A Course in Miracles, Foundation for Inner Peace, 448 Ignacio Blvd., #306, Novato, CA 94949, www..acim.org

Brown, Brene, www.brenebrown.com

Chodron, Pema, The Pema Chodron Foundation, 176 S. Dearborn Circle, Aurora, CO 80012, pemachodronfoundation.org

Dalton-Smith, Saundra, www.drdaltonsmith.com, support@ DrDaltonSmith.com

Danford, Staci, www.stacidanford.com. staci@thegratefulbrain.com

Dass, Ram, Love Serve Remember Foundation, 226 W Ojai Ave Ste 101#531, Ojai, CA 93023, www.ramdass.org

Dyer, Wayne, www.drwaynedyer.com

Edgar Cayce A.R.E., 215 67th Street, Virginia Beach, VA 23451, www.edgarcayce.org

Graham, Linda, Resources For Recovering Resilience, www.lindagraham-mft.net

Laughter Yoga, Nashik, MH – IND, www.laughteryoga.org, help@laughteryoga.org

One Spirit Learning Alliance, 2218 Broadway, New York, NY 10024, info@1spirit.org, www.1spirit.org

Robbins, Mel, Create a Better Life, www.melrobbins.com

The Intenders of the Highest Good, www.intenders.com

Tolle, Eckhart, www.eckharttolle.com, support@eckharttolle.com

Unity Worldwide Ministries, 200 Unity Circle North, Suite A, Lee's Summit, MO 64086, info@unity.org, www.unityworldwideministries.org

Walker, James Anthony, www.theartofjim.com

Wolfelt, Dr. Alan, Center for Loss & Life Transition, www.centerforloss.com